If you don't love books, you're going to love this book.

45 cards for all occasions, from extremely important to utterly pointless.

STERLING

New York / London
www.sterlingpublishing.com

STERLING and the distinctive Sterling logo, are registered trademarks of
Sterling Publishing Co., Inc.

10 9 8 7 6 5 4

Published by Sterling Publishing Co., Inc.
387 Park Avenue South, New York, NY 10016
© 2009 someecards, Inc.

Distributed in Canada by Sterling Publishing
C/o Canadian Manda Group, 165 Dufferin Street
Toronto, Ontario, Canada M6K 3H6
Distributed in the United Kingdom by GMC Distribution Services
Castle Place, 166 High Street, Lewes, East Sussex, England BN7 1XU
Distributed in Australia by Capricorn Link (Australia) Pty. Ltd.
P.O. Box 704, Windsor, NSW 2756, Australia

Printed in China
Sterling ISBN 978-1-4027-6808-8

For information about custom editions, special sales, premium and
corporate purchases, please contact Sterling Special Sales
Department at 800-805-5489 or specialsales@sterlingpublishing.com.

Contents

Introduction

If you like someecards.com, you're going to feel exactly the same or even better about the someecards book! This best-of collection is certain to make you look even more thoughtful, witty, caring, and obnoxious than you may already be. You can send these tear-out postcards to friends, relatives, coworkers, or anyone you just occasionally like to sleep with! Plus, think of all the time you're going to save this year by not having to sift through rack after rack of greeting cards that don't quite say what you want. With the someecards book, you won't need to stand up at all! While reclining, you can choose from a wide range of occasions for expressing exactly what you feel—everything from birthdays and anniversaries to simply telling someone you sort of remember they exist.

Too lazy to affix a stamp to something? Someecards is also the perfect coffee table book to impress houseguests. Not a fan of caffeine-related furniture or letting people in your home? Then use the cards as fun decor for your office, cubicle, dorm room, or brand new prison cell. There's no conceivable way to regret this purchase!

And if you genuinely dislike everything about the someecards book, including this introduction, why not give it to someone you're angry with in order to cause them pain? But don't just think of the someecards book as a way to exact revenge on mortal enemies—it's a great gift for friends, too! You simply can't go wrong with buying up to 17 copies of the someecards book.

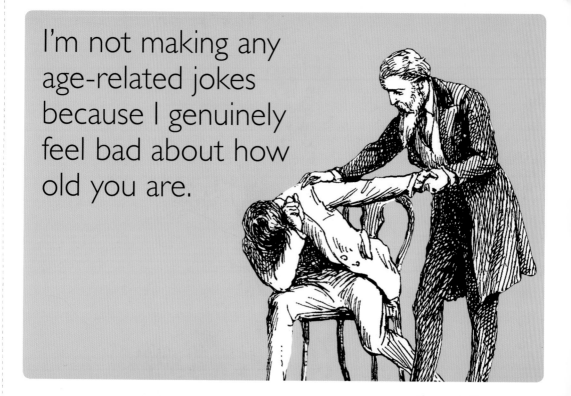

somee cards

May your birthday be devoid of cute animals and soul-shredding wordplay.

som<ee>cards

May you live long enough to shit yourself.

someecards

Today's the anniversary of you being expelled from your mother's uterus.

somee cards

Happy birthday to one of the few people whose birthday I can remember without a Facebook reminder.

som**ee**cards

I remember when you weren't so disturbingly old.

_____

_____

_____

_____

som**ee**cards

Let's over-celebrate
your birthday.

_____

_____

_____

_____

som**ee**cards

someecards

Wishing you a happy birthday makes me feel gay.

someecards

This is the perfect day to thank me for remembering your birthday.

_____

_____

_____

_____

som**ee**cards

Sorry in advance for doing a ton of stupid shit.

somee cards

somee cards

Sorry you don't understand how important I am.

somee cards

Congratulations on defying marriage statistics.

som**ee**cards

It's remarkable how long we've tolerated each other.

som**ee**cards

If I still had a soul,
you'd be its mate.

someⓔecards

Happy anniversary to a couple who almost never makes me physically ill.

som**ee**cards

someecards

Congratulations on finding your true calling.

someecards

Congratulations on ending your dry spell.

someecards

_____

_____

_____

_____

som**ee**cards

Sorry you're
feeling like such
a pussy.

someecards

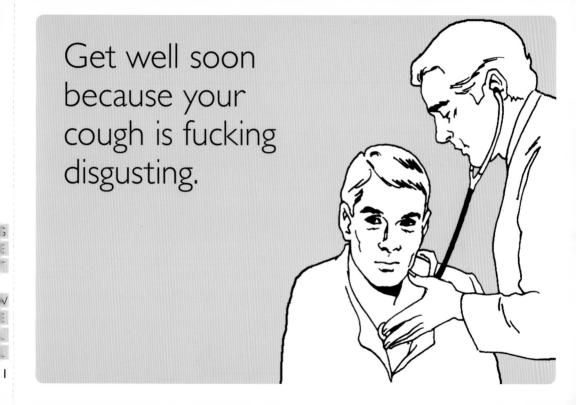

somee cards

Good luck finding shameful entry-level employment.

_____

_____

_____

_____

som**ee**cards

som ee cards

Congratulations on sleeping with the same person for the rest of eternity.

someecards

someecards

It would be
an honor to ruin
your wedding.

someecards

It's going to
be a great
first marriage.

som**ee**cards

I hope a mediocre Mother's Day brunch can help negate 364 days of smug ingratitude.

someecards

I love how we don't even need to say out loud that I'm your favorite child.

_____

_____

_____

_____

someecards

You're going to be a great MILF.

_____

_____

_____

_____

som ee cards

_____

_____

_____

_____

someecards

Thanks for being
a job reference
despite what
you know.

_____

_____

_____

_____

som**ee**cards

I think of you every
time I browse
my cell phone on
the toilet.

5

someecards

If I were ever to shoot you, it would just be in the leg.

_____

_____

_____

_____

som**ee**cards

We're total
fucking badasses.

_____

_____

_____

_____

som**ee**cards

I will be your friend no matter what you put inside your anus.

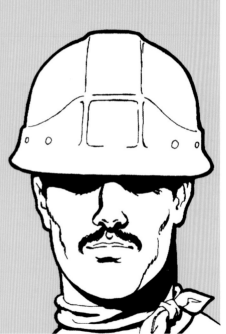

_____

_____

_____

_____

som**ee**cards

It's been too
long since we
threw up on
each other.

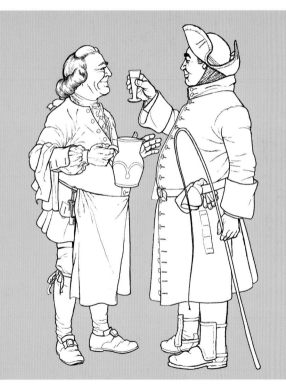

som**ee**cards

Our effortless friendship fits perfectly with my laziness.

someecards

I'd like to offer moral support but I have questionable morals.

_____

_____

_____

_____

som**ee**cards

When work feels
overwhelming,
remember that
you're going to die.

_____

_____

_____

_____

som**ee**cards

I'm outdoorsy in that I like getting drunk on patios.

_____

_____

_____

_____

someecards

My true love is out there somewhere and they can go fuck themselves.

someecards